The Business Of Being A CIO

How CIOs Can Use Their Technical Skills To Help Their Company Solve Real-World Business Problems

"Practical, proven techniques that will show you how to use technology to make your company more successful"

Dr. Jim Anderson

Published by:
Blue Elephant Consulting
Tampa, Florida

Copyright © 2014 by Dr. Jim Anderson

All rights reserved. No part of this book may be reproduced of transmitted in any form or by any means, electronic or mechanical, including photocopying, recording or by any information storage and retrieval system without written permission of the publisher, except for inclusion of brief quotations in a review.

Printed in the United States of America

Library of Congress Control Number: 2014920862

ISBN-13: 978-1503293434
ISBN-10: 1503293432

Warning – Disclaimer

The purpose of this book is to educate and entertain. This book does not promise or guarantee that anyone following the ideas, tips, suggestions, techniques or strategies will be successful. The author, publisher and distributor(s) shall have neither liability nor responsibility to anyone with respect to any loss or damage caused, or alleged to be caused, directly or indirectly by the information contained in this book.

Recent Books By The Author

Product Management

- How Product Managers Can Grow Their Career: How Product Managers Can Find And Succeed In The Right Job

- Product Management Secrets: Techniques For Product Managers To Boost Product Sales And Increase Customer Satisfaction

Public Speaking

- How To Organize A Successful Speech: How to put together a speech that will clearly communicate your message to your audience

- How To Become A Better Speaker By Changing How You Speak: Change techniques that will transform a speech into a memorable event

CIO Skills

- What CIOs Need To Know About Working With Partners: Techniques For CIOs To Use In Order To Be Able To Successfully Work With Partners

- How CIOs Can Make Innovation Happen: Tips And Techniques For CIOs To Use In Order To Make Innovation Happen In Their IT Department

IT Manager Skills

- How IT Managers Can Make Innovation Happen: Tips And Techniques For IT Managers To Use In Order To Make Innovation Happen In Their Teams

- Secrets Of Effective Leadership For IT Managers: Tips And Techniques That IT Managers Can Use In Order To Develop Leadership Skills

Negotiating

- Learn How To Signal In Your Next Negotiation: How To Develop The Skill Of Effective Signaling In A Negotiation In Order To Get The Best Possible Outcome

- Learn The Skill Of Exploring In A Negotiation: How To Develop The Skill Of Exploring What Is Possible In A Negotiation In Order To Reach The Best Possible Deal

Miscellaneous

- The Internet-Enabled Successful School District Superintendent: How To Use The Internet To Boost Parental Involvement In Your Schools

- Power Distribution Unit (PDU) Secrets: What Everyone Who Works In A Data Center Needs To Know!

Note: See a complete list of books by Dr. Jim Anderson at the back of this book.

Acknowledgements

Any book like this one is the result of years of real-world work experience. In my over 25 years of working for 7 different firms, I have met countless fantastic people and I've been mentored by some truly exceptional ones. Although I've probably forgotten some of the people who made me the person that I am today, here is my attempt to finally give them the recognition that they so truly deserve:

- Thomas P. Anderson
- Art Puett
- Bobbi Marshall
- Bob Boggs

Dr. Jim Anderson

This book is dedicated to my family: Lori, Maddie, Nick, and Ben. None of this would have been possible without their constant love and support.

Thanks for always believing in me and providing me with the strength to always be willing to go out there and be my best for you.

Table Of Contents

TECHNOLOGY THAT EVERY CIO NEEDS TO KNOW ABOUT 8

ABOUT THE AUTHOR...9

CHAPTER 1: STALL ALERT! HOW AN IT DEPARTMENT CAN HELP 14

CHAPTER 2: A GEEK'S GUIDE TO THE FINANCIAL MELT-DOWN.........18

CHAPTER 3: 10 WAYS THAT IT CAN SOLVE REAL-WORLD BUSINESS PROBLEMS 27

CHAPTER 4: NO BUBBLE HERE: IT SPENDING GOING UP NEXT YEAR!32

CHAPTER 5: ARE CIOS LOOKING DOWN WHEN THEY SHOULD BE LOOKING UP?..36

CHAPTER 6: WHAT SHOULD A CIO'S TOP 10 CONCERNS BE RIGHT NOW? 40

CHAPTER 7: WE'RE IN A RECESSION, WHAT'S AN IT DEPARTMENT TO DO?..45

CHAPTER 8: DOES IHOP HAVE TASTY LESSONS TO SERVE UP FOR IT? 49

CHAPTER 9: CAN WE MAKE IT ANY MORE COMPLEX THAN IT IS?.....53

CHAPTER 10: WELCOME TO A NEW YEAR: DOES IT MATTER THIS YEAR? 57

CHAPTER 11: 3 WAYS TO FIX AN IT DEPARTMENT (SUGGESTIONS FROM EUROPE) 63

CHAPTER 12: HOW CAN YOU MAKE YOUR IT DEPARTMENT STRATEGIC?..67

The Business Of Being A CIO

All too often CIOs can get caught up in all of the technical details of the job: boosting uptime, replacing servers, guarding against cyber criminals, etc. What we tend to forget is that IT exists to serve the rest of the business and they are there (in most cases) to make money. This means that there needs to be a business side to IT and that is one of a CIO's key responsibilities.

The business is always facing a set of business problems. What you need to do as a CIO is to take the time to understand how these problems appear to the rest of the company. Then you need to use your technical skills to identify ways that the IT department can help the company solve these problems.

This is going to have a huge impact on how you accomplish your CIO job. Your focus is going to have to shift from your department to watching over the rest of the company. Your top concerns are going to have to be business based, not technology based.

In order to be a successful business based CIO, you need to establish clear lines of communication with the rest of the departments in the company. This means that the way that you talk about IT is going to have to change. No longer can you use the technical shorthand lingo that is used within IT, instead you are going to have to simplify things for everyone else.

In the end it has to be your goal to transform the IT department. Gone are the days when you could simply be a support arm of the company fixing email systems and laptops. Now you need to become the strategic partner that the rest of the firm is going to have to rely on in order to accomplish their business goals.

This book has been written in order to provide you with an understanding of how you can use your technical skills to solve business problems for your company. Follow the suggestions in this book and you'll transform your IT department into a powerful competitive tool for the rest of the firm to use.

For more information on what it takes to be a great CIO, check out my blog, The Accidental Successful CIO, at:

www.TheAccidentalSuccessfulCIO.com

Good luck!

- Dr. Jim Anderson

About The Author

I must confess that I never set out to be a CIO. When I went to school, I studied Computer Science and thought that I'd get a nice job programming and that would be that. Well, at least part of that plan worked out!

My first job was working for Boeing on their F/A-18 fighter jet program. I spent my days programming fighter jet software in assembly language and I loved it. The U.S. government decided to save some money and went looking for other countries to sell this plane to. This put me into an unfamiliar role: I started to meet with foreign military officials and I ended up having to manage groups of engineers who were working on international projects.

Time moved on and so did I. I found myself working for Siemens, the big German telecommunications company. They were making phone switches and selling them to the seven U.S. phone companies. The problem was that the switches were too complicated. Customers couldn't tell the difference between one complicated phone switch from another complicated phone switch. Once again I found myself working with the sales and marketing teams to find ways to make the great technology that the engineers had developed understandable to both internal and external customers.

I've spent over 25 years working as an senior IT professional for both big companies and startups. This has given me an opportunity to learn what it takes to manage and IT department in ways that allow it to maximize its output while becoming a valuable part of the overall company.

I now live in Tampa Florida where I spend my time managing my consulting business, Blue Elephant Consulting, teaching college courses at the University of South Florida, and traveling to work with companies like yours to share the knowledge that I have about how to create and manage successful IT departments.

I'm always available to answer questions and I can be reached at:

Dr. Jim Anderson
Blue Elephant Consulting
Email: jim@BlueElephantConsulting.com
Facebook: http://goo.gl/1TVoK
Web: **www.BlueElephantConsulting.com**

"Unforgettable communication skills that will set your ideas free..."

Create IT Departments That Are Productive And A Valuable Asset To The Rest Of The Company !

Dr. Jim Anderson is available to provide training and coaching on the topics that are the most important to people who have to manage IT departments: how can I build a productive IT department (and keep it together) while at the same time providing the rest of the company with the IT services that they need?

Dr. Anderson believes that in order to both learn and remember what he says, speakers need to laugh. Each one of his speeches is full of fun and humor so that what he says "sticks" with everyone.

Dr. Anderson's CIO Skills Training Includes:

1. How to identify and attract the right type of IT workers to your IT department.
2. How to build relationships with the company's senior management in order to get the support that you need?
3. How to stay on top of changing technology and security issues so that you never get surprised?

Dr. Jim Anderson works with over 100 customers per year. To invite Dr. Anderson to work with you, contact him at:

Phone: 813-418-6970 or
Email: jim@BlueElephantConsulting.com

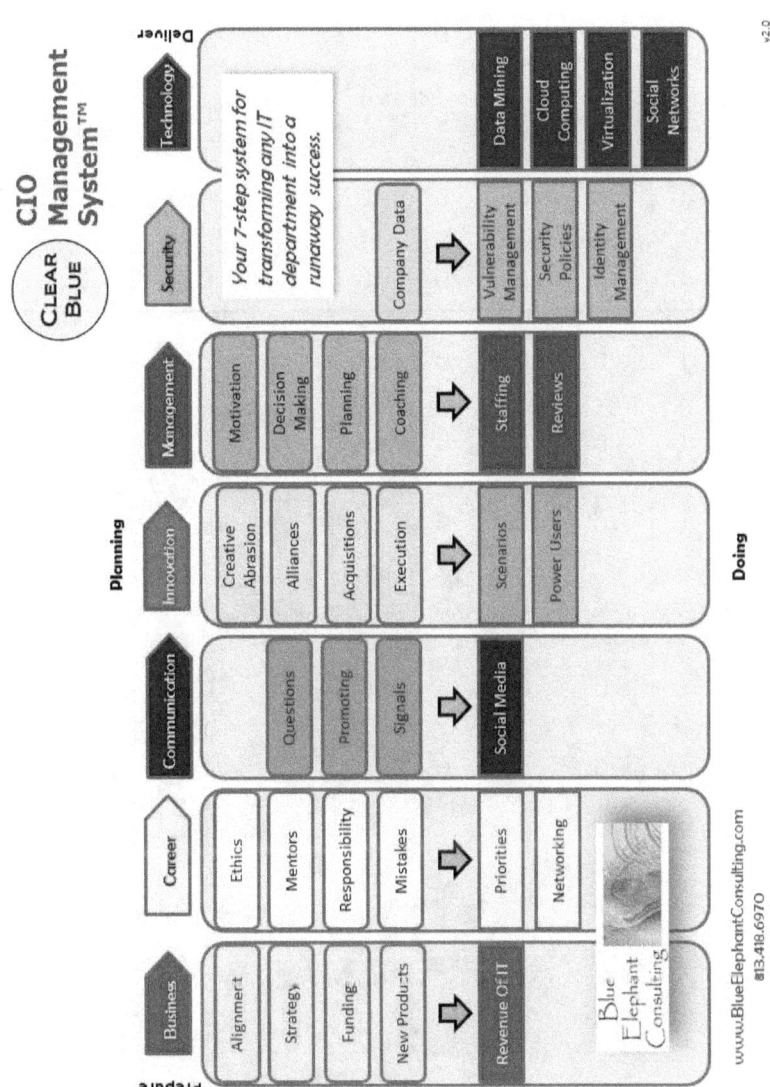

The **Clear Blue CIO Management System™** has been created to provide CIOs and senior IT managers with a clear roadmap for how to manage an IT department. This system shows CIOs what needs to be done and in what order to do it.

Chapter 1

Stall Alert! How An IT Department Can Help

Chapter 1: Stall Alert! How An IT Department Can Help

Companies can get blindsided by entering an economic stall that they never saw coming. As a CIO, you need a quick overview of some steps that an IT department can take in order to help prevent the company from coming to grief.

We'll be talking about four different strategies that have been used by management teams in the past. The first two are designed to make a company's strategic assumptions explicit to everyone. The next two are designed to test those assumptions in order to determine if they are still accurate and relevant. Here they are:

- **Create an IT Core-Belief Inquisition Squad:** Since how the IT department operates has such a significant impact on the overall health of the company, create a cross-functional team to go on a fact-finding mission to collect the department's most closely held beliefs about itself and the firm that it is supporting. The shorter the tenure of the members of the team, the better because it will help to avoid too much belief in how things are currently done.

    The goal of the team should be to raise the issues that no one wants to talk about and to challenge the beliefs that everyone takes for granted: what industry is the company in? Who are IT's customers? What are 10 things that you would never hear our customers say about IT? Are our competitors' IT departments more valuable than us?

- **Invent A Pre-Mortum Strategic Analysis:** This activity consists of an off-site meeting where participants imagine what the future will be like in 5 years and how the IT department will have contributed to the success or failure of the company as a whole.

The key to this exercise is to identify the issues and factors that various success/failure scenarios have in common. Once this is known, then the IT leaders can identify a set of core IT beliefs and take the time to both examine and monitor them.

- **Create A Shadow CIO & IT Team:** This is the most dangerous of the four practices. If you want to be able to get a different view of the same information, create a "B-Team" of high-potential IT managers who will eventually be promoted.

    Have the briefings that will be given to the CIO and his direct reports given to them the day before and have the shadow team discuss the issues and search for answers. Have a scribe attend and note the flow of the discussion, the issues raised, and the conclusions reached. The two benefits that this brings are that it prepares the next wave of IT leaders before they are promoted and it provides a fresh perspective on how issues and solutions can be viewed.

- **Bring A Venture Capitalist To The Table:** The challenge here is that someone needs to find a venture capitalist with some time to spare. However, if you can do that, then they can be a huge asset in probing the IT strategy for weaknesses. A VC will challenge any and all IT positions and will be able to provide a very practical, payback focused view of the IT strategy.

    The VC views the world in terms of making each decision to fund optional – additional funding is only provided if specific milestones have already been met.

Why bother with these four practices – after all they sure seem like a lot of effort? The simple fact is that once an economic stall hits a company, the data shows that the longer the stall exists, the better the probability that the company will never recover.

As the world of business continues to speed up. researchers believe that there will be an increase in the number of firms that enter into a stall in the future. The tools that we've discussed here provide the IT department with a way to help the company detect and then avoid a stall.

Chapter 2

A Geek's Guide To The Financial Melt-Down

Chapter 2: A Geek's Guide To The Financial Melt-Down

Man – what a mess! There for a while I was almost afraid to unwrap the paper each morning because the font size of the headlines seems to be getting bigger and bigger as the financial news got worse and worse. Stock trading firms were going belly up, others were getting bought. Fannie Mae and Freddie Mac (who are they?) got taken over by the government and then WaMu failed. Clearly this was the end of the world. Maybe.

As a reasonably gifted technical person, I thought that I knew how the world of finance worked (and so to apparently did a lot of people who worked in finance); however, with the wheels coming off of the truck, now I'm not so sure. I really needed someone to explain to me just how so much could go so wrong so quickly. And that's where Stephen stepped in.

Stephen Schwarzman is a true Master of the Universe in financial circles. First off, he's a billionaire. Secondly, he's the chairman and co-founder of the Blackstone Group private-equity firm. In case you aren't aware of it, Blackstone is HUGE and they only play with numbers that end in "Billion". So when the Wall Street Journal and the Yale School of Management hosted a round table of important people in finance, he was there.

Stephen started what was intended to be a Q&A session with an (almost) all-in-one-breath summary of just what the heck has happened to the financial markets. For geeks who like their technical information short & sweet and preferably from a guru, you're not going to get much better than this. Here's the whole quote:

> *It's a perfect storm. It started with Congress encouraging lending to lower income people. You went*

> *from subprime loans being 2% of total loans in 2002 to 30% of total loans in 2006. That kind of enormous increase swept into a net people who shouldn't have been borrowing.*
>
> *Those loans were packaged into CDOs rated AAA, which lead to the investment-banking firms [buying them] to do little to no due diligence and the securities were distributed throughout the world where they started defaulting.*
>
> *When they started defaulting, out of bad luck or bad judgment, we implemented fair-value accounting... You had wildly different marks for this kind of security, which led to massive write-offs by the commercial-banking and investment-banking system.*
>
> *In the face of those losses... you needed to raise new equity...which came from sovereign-wealth funds, in part, which then caused political resistance to sovereign-wealth funds, who predictably have withdrawn from putting money into the system... It seemed pretty obvious that would have to happen. We now find ourselves with a liquidity crisis where fundamentally the cost of money for financial intermediaries [such as investment banks] is significantly in excess of their cost of lending it. So several institutions found themselves in a structurally impossible position... Goldman reverted to a banking charter for a lower cost of funds, which today is still not low enough for the business. So that is the story of how we got here.*

Whew! All that in one breath? The man truly knows his stuff. If you got all of that, then you can stop reading now and you are fully prepared to be the star of the next cocktail party that you go to this week. However, if like me some of what Stephen said sailed over your head, then let's take a few moments and do some debugging and see what he was really getting at. Maybe if we step through what he said line-by-line it will make more sense:

> *It's a perfect storm. It started with Congress encouraging lending to lower income people. You went from subprime loans being 2% of total loans in 2002 to 30% of total loans in 2006. That kind of enormous increase swept into a net people who shouldn't have been borrowing.*

Congress enacted the Community Reinvestment Act (CRA) in 1977 in order to encourage banks to extend loans to qualified people with low incomes. Home loans are actually divided into four different categories: prime, jumbo, subprime and near-prime mortgages. Everything is based on your credit risk: if you have a stable job and a good credit rating, then you can get a prime mortgage (lower interest rate). Jumbo loans are generally of prime quality, but they exceed the $417,000 ceiling for mortgages that can be bought and guaranteed by government-sponsored enterprises – basically if you are buying a McMansion then this is the kind of loan you'd take out. Near-prime mortgages are made at a higher interest rate than prime, but lower than subprime. These are for folks who may not be able to document their income or may have trouble providing a down payment. Subprime loans are for folks with poor credit ratings and risky sources of income. These loans carry the highest interest rates.

Things percolated along quite nicely and non-prime loans made up about 9% of all home loans being made up through about 2001. Then BANG! Two things happened: some clever mortgage banker devils decided to change how they calculated a person's credit worthiness – they started using the same rules that were used to get auto loans (these were looser rules – it was much easier to get a loan). But wait, there's more! By itself, just making it easier to qualify for a home loan would not have been enough to cause subprime loans to surge from 9% to 40% of all home loans being made in 2006. There had to be something else...

Once again, it was clever bankers to the rescue. See, it turns out that in order for a bank to make a loan, they need to have equity capital on hand to back those loans up (that's what they are loaning out). When you run out of this, you've got to stop making loans and that means that you'll miss out on making all that money that banks make when they process mortgages (remember all those "fees" when you bought a house?). What banks really like to do is to sell a mortgage to investors after they've completed the paperwork. This way it's off their books and they've got more money to loan out. Hmm, the problem was that these subprime mortgages were too risky to sell to traditional investors. What to do? Sure seems like it's time to invent a new financial vehicle to take care of this.

> *Those loans were packaged into CDOs rated AAA, which lead to the investment-banking firms [buying them] to do little to no due diligence and the securities were distributed throughout the world where they started defaulting.*

Oh, oh – it's vocabulary time. Remember, banks made prime mortgages funded with deposits from savers (you and me) and then sold them to investors. Near-prime and subprime mortgages presented a bit of a problem – no investor was going to touch them because they were too risky. This is where CDOs come in.

A **Collateralized Debt Obligations (CDO)** is a clever investment tool that was created to make investing in subprime mortgages easier for investors to stomach. What happens is that a lot of subprime mortgages were sold by banks and mortgage originators (non-banks that were handing out mortgages) and then these loans were stuck together into a CDO. Inside a CDO, individual loans were placed into one of three "trenches": senior (pretty safe), mezzanine (sorta safe), and equity / unrated (uhh – I'm not so sure about this). Each trench paid a different interest rate with the higher risk trenches paying more to compensate investors for the higher risk. Got it so far?

What Stephen is talking about is that this all sorta works if there is a mix of loans (good/bad/ugly) in a CDO. What happens if they are all ugly? It turns out that these beasts are fairly complex and it's quite difficult to accuracy determine how risky one of them is. The guys who are supposed to be good at doing this, the credit rating agencies (Moody's, Standard & Poor's), apparently were asleep at the wheel. An "AAA" rating basically means that an investment is a "sure thing" – it's rock solid. They classified a lot of CDOs as being AAA when they were really made up of too many subprime mortgages. Oh oh!

Things starting hitting the fan when folks started missing their mortgage payments on their subprime loans. This resulted in default rates shooting up. Hold on – this is where things start to get bad. Defaulting subprime loans then started to cause CDOs that were based on them to stop generating returns to investors (if nobody is making their monthly loan payments, then there is nothing to pass on to investors). All the clever tricks that had been set up to make sure that CDOs could withstand some defaults crumbled when it turned out that lots of CDOs were made up of all high risk subprime loans.

> *When they started defaulting, out of bad luck or bad judgment, we implemented fair-value accounting... You had wildly different marks for this kind of security, which led to massive write-offs by the commercial-banking and investment-banking system.*

So the sky started falling. What made things get so bad so quickly? Well this little accounting trick called fair-value accounting sure didn't help things. What this means is that the value of a CDO is based on the current market price for that CDO (whatever someone is willing to pay you for it right now). When the financial world started to turn upside down and the loans that made up lots of CDOs started to turn out to be worthless, that meant that the value of the CDO itself started a race to $0. This is what caused the U.S. government to have to step in and save Fannie Mae and Freddie Mac: they were backing too many bad loans.

When you are an investor and your investment has become worthless overnight (ouch!), what do you do? You write it off – you tell the world that your gold has become lead and you've just lost a lot of money. This happens all the time and everyone hopes to move on and do better next time. However, this time around lenders reacted to these signs by tightening credit standards especially on riskier mortgages.

When it became hard for everyone (prime, subprime, etc.) to get loans, people stopped buying houses. This meant that it became much harder to sell a house. This meant that if you got behind in your house payments then you couldn't just sell the house and make yourself whole. You basically HAD to default on your loan and just walk away.

This meant that the banks and financial institutions could no longer raise money they way that they had been doing even as their investments turned to dust. Can you say cash flow problem? The perfect storm had arrived.

> *In the face of those losses... you needed to raise new equity...which came from sovereign-wealth funds, in part, which then caused political resistance to sovereign-wealth funds, who predictably have withdrawn from putting money into the system... It seemed pretty obvious that would have to happen.*

So if you are a Lehman Brothers, what do you do now? You start clutching at straws. Your next best source of cash is what is called a Sovereign Wealth Funds (SWF). SWFs are typically created when governments have budgetary surpluses and have little or no international debt. A good example of a SWF is the Kuwait Investment Authority – lots of money looking for a home that will generate more money.

Having foreign governments make big investments in the firms that control big parts of the U.S. economy made our elected officials in Washington D.C. very nervous. To make themselves feel better, they passed the Foreign Investment and National Security Act of 2007. Basically, this gave the government veto power over any deal that involved a SWF. The SWFs said, ok – if you are going to be that way, then we'll go play somewhere else. If you were WaMu, then you just saw your last best chance for funding to save yourself walk away!

After this, everything just went to hell in a handbag. However, here's the final take away that Stephen didn't cover. Everything will work out in the end. What needs to happen is that the credit markets that businesses and people borrow from have to unfreeze. Once this happens, then people will start borrowing again (rationally we hope). Then investors will return and start to make investments. Life will once again get back to normal. Grit your teeth and we'll get through this together.

Chapter 3

10 Ways That IT Can Solve Real-World Business Problems

Chapter 3: 10 Ways That IT Can Solve Real-World Business Problems

My favorite word is "alignment". This describes the situation that happens when an IT department gets it act together and focuses on solving problems for the business. This is actually different from what an IT department normally spends its time doing: keeping the network up and providing help desk support for end users.

The folks over at eWeek found out that a number of IT departments have actually been listening to what the rest of the business has been asking for and they are now starting to create custom solutions that solve real-world business problems.

The IT departments have been starting with the single app that has the most valuable information in it, the Customer Relationship Management (CRM) application, and then extending it to do useful work. How about if we take a look at 10 of these applications:

1. **Where's My Trash (Truck):** An Atlanta based company called Trash-It has combined their Microsoft Dynamics CRM Live tool with the Tom-Tom Work application, a GPS navigation tool. This now allows the business side of the house to see where all of their trash trucks are at any time and better manage and control the fleet. Instead of guessing if they have too many or too few trucks, now they know!

2. **Helping Out The Homeless**: San Francisco's Family Service Agency has the nearly impossible task of running six major helping centers with over 250 staff members. On a yearly basis, they are able to help 8,000 clients. They had a huge problem: how could they tell who they had served and where they had served them?

If they knew this, then they could better coordinate their services and make the best use of their limited funding. Their IT department used Salesforce.com's Force.com platform to build a single integrated record for each client. This allowed the business side of the house, six different agencies, to view each customer's single record of service.

3. **Conserve More:** The U.S. Department of Agriculture does a lot of conservation work. Until now, different systems had been used to track different conservation projects. Their IT department used Microsoft's Dynamic CRM 4.0 to build a conservation work tracking application. Now the rest of the department is able to view all of the conservation efforts in a single place.

4. **Is There A Doctor Here?**: The good folks at the Schumacher Group are responsible for providing both doctors and operating teams to over 140 hospitals that are spread out over multiple states. This works out ok if everything is going fine; however, in the event of a natural disaster it can become very difficult to find doctors and get them to where they are most urgently needed. The IT team used Salesforce.com's Force.com platform to create a hurricane tracking app that integrates doctor location information. This allows the business side of the house to swing into action when disaster strikes and make sure that the right resources are sent to the right locations.

5. **Geek Map**: The Geeks On The Way service found that business was just a little bit too good. Their employees were spending way too much time trying to map service calls so that they could provide the most efficient service to their spread out customer base. Their IT department (yes, Geeks need an IT department also) used the SugarCRM app to create an application that

automatically linked with the open source Asterisk PBX phone system and map out routes for their techs to use for service calls.

6. **Super Bowl Story**: The company Total Structures has what I consider to be a fun job – they are in the business of building custom structures. Where this story gets interesting is when you realize that they won the job to build the halftime stage that was used at this year's Super Bowl (yep, we all saw it for about 30 minutes, but I'll bet none of us can remember what it looked like!) You can imagine just how complex building a structure that has to magically show up, be used, and then vanish must be. Their IT department used Microsoft Dynamics CRM Live to come up with an application that they could use to track the building of the stage. Now how's that for stretching the definition of a CRM application!

7. **HIPPA-Hurray, HIPPA-Hurray!**: The Department of Human Services out in Oregon had a real problem on their hands. They were trying to manage Medicaid claims that they were receiving from over 35,000 health care providers in the state. This meant that they were dealing with 60,000 paper-based claims each month. Oh, and the new HIPPA rules were coming into effect. Their IT department used the SugarCRM app to move to electronic forms. As a nice side-benefit, they became HIPPA compliant along the way.

8. **It's All About Politics**: No matter what side of the political fence you sit on, you've got to admire former presidential candidate Mitt Rommney's campaign team. Their IT folks used Salesforce.com's Force.com platform to create an app that allowed volunteers to get info out to those who needed it while at the same time using emails to ask for campaign funds. How successful was

this app? Well by using it Mitt Rommney was able to raise $20M for his bid. He lost, but still that's a lot of money!

9. **You Are In Germany:** The Kassel region over in Germany decided to use the SugarCRM app to get more folks to visit them. They designed a social networking platform that was designed to attract all sorts of people: tourists, businesses, and even people who might want to move to Kassel.

10. **Tracking School Days**: So this last one doesn't really involve an IT department; however, it still struck me as being a very cool app. The Bronx Lab School wanted to be able to both measure and track individual student performance. They decided to use Salesforce.com's Force.com app to build a tool that would let them track student performance. The very cool part is that it delivers daily updates on each student to advisers, teachers, and (of course) parents.

What I hope that you take away from this short list of novel applications is that it is possible for an IT shop to get a seat at a company's strategic planning table. All it takes is some careful thinking about what the business is trying to accomplish and the focused application of good 'ol IT skills to solve those business problems.

Chapter 4

No Bubble Here: IT Spending Going Up Next Year!

Chapter 4: No Bubble Here: IT Spending Going Up Next Year!

As the rest of the world seems to be going through some sort of complete meltdown, the IT industry is in the process of holding its breath. 2001 was not all that long ago and we can remember what happened back then all too well: days of unlimited spending, lots of travel, and lavish celebrations came to a screeching halt almost overnight as the banks cut off credit and the IT bubble popped.

Reading the newspapers and watching TV one would be lead to believe that the same sort of doom and gloom seems to be settling over all industries right now. Is another bubble popping what they mean by Internet 2.0?

Well the folks over at Gartner have some (basically) good news for you. They've been talking with everyone and their mother's brother and what they have found out is that YES, IT spending is going to get cut back because of all of the financial turmoil that is currently going on. However, we're not going to see the massive cutbacks that came after the dot.com bust.

Before the subprime fueled meltdown of the financial markets started to happen, Gartner had been predicting that spending on IT for next year was going to increase at a healthy 5.8%. To put this in perspective, you've got to realize that during the dot.com era, IT spending lived in the middle double digits. However, after the bust happened, IT spending descended into the basement of low single digit growth (less than inflation!) and remained there for several years. Gartner's new guess for IT spending next year is (drum roll please) 2.3%.

Peter Sondergaard is Gartner's global head of research. He believes that IT spending generally lags behind the general economy by at least two quarters, so the current meltdown won't impact IT spending until roughly mid next year.

What's going to get cut? Sondergaard says that hardware spending is an easy hit – it will probably get curtailed earlier and harder than either software or IT services. Spending on those IT services should probably focus on off-shore outsourcing. What's interesting is that they aren't predicting any more really big, big deals. Instead you should expect to see a collection of smaller outsourcing deals.

The folks in the software industry have cleverly thought to set up sorta of a "safety net" for themselves should this kind of contraction occur. Most software vendors (Oracle, SAP, Microsoft, etc.) have gotten their customers to sign up for long term support contacts so they may be able to dance by any general market slowdown with minimal impacts.

In IT it generally takes us about 10 years to adopt a new technology. This time around, the experts are thinking that the downturn may cause everyone to adopt new technology faster because it will result in big cost savings just when they are needed the most. Expect Software as a Service (SaaS) and so-called Cloud Computing services to be among the early winners from this situation.

Chapter 5

Are CIOs Looking Down When They Should Be Looking Up?

Chapter 5: Are CIOs Looking Down When They Should Be Looking Up?

Rob Preston over at Information Week was talking about some interesting CIO studies that were done recently and what they show is that it looks like CIOs are not spending their time where they should be. As the U.S. (and the rest of the world!) sufferers through a financial downturn, you'd think that everyone would be trying to show just how valuable they are to the company. Sadly, in the case of CIOs it doesn't look like this is happening...

The surveys of CIOs showed that "IT / Business Alignment" is still a top priority for CIOs. Now what makes this interesting is that this has been on the top of CIOs to-do list for a very long time. Preston makes the point that he is hoping that internal alignment between IT shops and their business counterparts has already occurred.

He is hoping that what CIOs are talking about is taking IT / business alignment to the next step and extending it down the supplier path and perhaps even reaching out to align with the customer. I hear his frustration; however, I don't think that internal alignment has actually occurred yet, but more about that later on.

One of the pieces of good news that came from the survey of CIOs was that items such as "IT strategic planning" have moved up CIOs to-do list. The hope is that if IT departments are involved in these types of activities, then as things get tighter due to the economic downturn IT funding won't be slashed as much as it has been in the past. When IT projects are seen as "nice to have" instead of "must have", it's far easier for a firm to take money away from an IT department.

The biggest concern that came out of the two CIO surveys that Preston talks about are how the CIOs identified how their departments were contributing to the overall success of their firms. You would be hoping to hear some solid business thinking here; however, that was not the case.

Instead, traditional IT tasks such as maintaining existing systems, ensuring network operation, deploying large-scale systems, reducing costs by automating processes, etc. were on their list. If you read though this list with a careful eye, you'll notice that any one of these tasks could be done by an outsourcing firm just as well as a captive IT shop.

What does all of this mean? To put it simply, CIOs get that they need to do a better job of becoming part of the business. When they think long term, they are working to figure out how they can make their IT department help the business to succeed.

However, the problem comes in the short term. Too many IT departments are focused on doing what they have always been doing – the comfortable stuff. The problem seems to be that nobody, CIOs included, really knows how to get from here (present time) to there (IT / business alignment nirvana). That's sorta sad because the steps are pretty clear to me. They start out like this:

1. **Business Wins:** IT needs to accept that it needs to become more like the rest of the business, not the other way around. IT is just one department, the rest of the business is much bigger and they make the money. Enough said.

2. **Subject Matter Experts Rule:** IT staff needs to spend some serious time learning everything that they can about the business that they are working in. No matter if you work with food, drugs, cars, or glass, everyone in IT needs to understand how that industry operates from top to bottom.

3. **Learn To Make Life Easier For The Business:** IT exists to make life easier for the business – so show it! Specifically, IT should understand how the business runs so that it can identify and automate the business processes that slow the business down.

4. **Speak The Language Of Business:** Develop the ability to speak the language of the industry! This is how the rest of the company communicates and it's high time that the IT department gets on board. Stop talking about version control, requirements gathering, maintenance upgrades, server consolidation because the rest of the company doesn't have a clue what you are talking about. Instead talk about revenue, customer retention, driving sales growth, and bottom line results.

Hopefully the next time a bunch of CIOs are surveyed, they'll have the right set of "looking up" priorities that are being used to manage their short term actions.

Chapter 6

What Should A CIO's Top 10 Concerns Be Right Now?

Chapter 6: What Should A CIO's Top 10 Concerns Be Right Now?

Let's take a quick snapshot of the business world as it stands right now: uncertainties (and hope) about a new president coming in, financial markets don't seem to be responding to stimulus programs, gas is down to $2.00 / gallon but for how long, and Paris Hilton hasn't been hear from for most of the summer.

Hmm, is this the best of times or the worst of times? What should a CIO be worrying about right now? Doing more outsourcing? Picking the best time to upgrade the company to Windows 10? Virtualizing more servers? NO! None of those are things that a CIO should be worrying about right now. The CIO should have a laser-like focus on the very same things that the CFO is worried about. Oh, oh. So what is the CFO worried about right now?

If you want to know what CFOs are staying up nights worrying about, then you've got to ask them. Thankfully for us this job has been taken care of for us by the Duke University / CFO magazine Global Business Outlook Survey.

CFOs are very afraid that credit issues are going to be rippling through the supply chains that their firms use. This means that the boys and girls in finance are worried that suppliers won't be able to supply and customers won't be able to pay. Oh, and the CFOs' companies may not be able to get access to the capital funds that they need also. So what are the top 10 concerns of today's CFOs? Here they are:

CFO Top External Concerns:

1. Consumer Demand
2. Credit markets / interest rates

3. Housing-market fallout
4. Cost of fuel
5. Cost of nonfuel commodities
6. Upcoming change in the U.S. administration
7. Other
8. Financial regulation
9. Devaluation of the U.S. dollar
10. Environmental regulation
11. International political stability

This of course brings up the key question: what are CIOs doing to decrease their CFO's fears of these issues? Case in point would be the cost of fuel. Although prices have slid for now, we all know that they can go back up just as easily. The CIO should be coming up with technology based solutions to implement "smart buildings" so that office energy usage can be monitored and minimized. Tracking of fleet vehicles and optimization of delivery and pickup schedules can also result in massive savings – just look to UPS for an example of this.

As they like to say on television, but wait – there's more! Those were just the top external concerns of CFOs. What are their top INTERNAL concerns?

CFO Top Internal, Company-Specific Concerns

1. Cost and availability of nonfinancial labor
2. Ability to forecast results
3. Cost of health care
4. Supply-chain risk
5. Other
6. Data security
7. Cost and availability of labor in accounting / finance
8. Auditing

Once again, the CIO should be jumping on the ability to forecast results. This problem calls out for a technology based solution for creating, tracking, and updating forecasts. Additionally, reducing the turn-over in the IT department staff can go a long way towards minimizing hiring and training costs for the firm as a whole.

In the end, IT exists to serve the needs of the company. Yes, planning a company-wide upgrade to Windows 10 is important; however, this is not what the CFO is worried about. In order for the CIO to have a seat at the table when the strategic direction of the company is being planned, then the CFOs top concerns need to be the CIOs top concerns.

Chapter 7

We're In A Recession, What's An IT Department To Do?

Chapter 7: We're In A Recession, What's An IT Department To Do?

Remember what happened to the IT industry back in 2001? When the dot.com bubble burst, pretty much the sky started falling and IT spending hit the proverbial brick wall. If you've been reading the newspapers or watching TV lately, then you've probably noticed that the global economic downturn sure looks like what we saw back in 2001. Should an IT department be worried?

The good folks over at Forester Research have just released a forecast. When they looked into their crystal balls, they saw that this year's IT spending will grow at its lowest rate in the past six years.

IT spending will actually still increase just a wee bit – it will grow to be 1.6% more than they spent in last year. This will be a change from the past two years because IT budgets had grown by 4.1% and 7% in the two previous years.

The reason that IT budgets will still grow just a bit this year even though the rest of the world is shrinking is because the world has changed – businesses have grown so dependent on IT that they can't help but spend as much or more than they did the year before.

For those of us who remember the dot.com crash (myself included), we shouldn't be too worried about IT spending taking the long lasting nose dive that it did back in 2001.

The reason that things are different this time is because back in the dot.com days firms had overinvested in IT systems and staff. The thinking is that this time around IT departments have been running a much leaner shop for the past few years and so they won't have to cut as deep as other departments may have to.

So what's an IT department to do in this down cycle? Focusing on helping the firm to cut costs is one way that IT can help now and build good will for use later on.

A relatively simple project to consider is switching your corporate email system from an in-house system to an external on-line provider. Yes, email is a critical business application; however, it's not unique to your business. Having your expensive IT teams spending time on keeping the email system up and running is taking away from other business specific work that they could be doing.

If your business is the creation and selling of software products, then you should be cautious going forward. Forrester's study found that software revenue is predicted to grow at only 3.4% in this year. Additionally, most of this growth will be coming not from new product sales but rather from support fees from previous purchases of software.

What everyone needs to realize is that right now nobody is spending any time planning for the future. This is a luxury that IT departments cannot afford to take. When the global economy snaps back, IT is once again going to be expected to start driving company profits!

Chapter 8

Does IHOP Have Tasty Lessons To Serve Up For IT?

Chapter 8: Does IHOP Have Tasty Lessons To Serve Up For IT?

I don't know about you, but I'm always open to having breakfast no matter what time of day it is. This might explain why so much of my life has been spent sitting in IHOP restaurants eating mountains of pancakes. When I stumbled across an interview with IHOP's CIO in eWeek magazine, I was of course interested...

Patrick Piccininno became IHOP's CIO way back in 2003. He's got some interesting thoughts on what it takes to get and keep a CIO as a part of a company's strategy team. Piccininno agrees that just to get the CIO a seat at the table has been a long fought battle.

He believes that in order for a CIO to keep his/her seat at the table, they need to make sure that they are not a wallflower – they actually have to be a participating member in planning the corporate strategy and they need to be willing to work with the CEO and the other members of the executive team.

Here's the key take-away for all of us IT lovers: Piccininno states that in his experience, a CIO needs to take off his/her technology hat and instead put on their business hat. When working with other members of the executive team it's critical the that CIO focus on those transformational initiatives that will help the company to achieve its business results.

Piccininno believes that what the rest of the company really wants from the IT department is to simply believe that they are in good hands – that the IT infrastructure will support whatever needs to be done to grow the business.

I think that we've all heard this kind of talk before, but it can be very difficult to understand exactly how to put it into effect in the real world. Piccininno offered an example that provided a good case study.

Back in July of 2007, IHOP announced that it was going to buy the Applebee's restaurant chain. This was a big deal – it was valued at about US$2.1B. As Piccininno points out, a key part of the decision to go ahead and buy Applebee's rested on the ability of the IHOP IT department to be able to successfully integrate two sets of disparate systems and environments quickly in order to reduce costs.

In order for IHOP's IT department to be able to support this large scale merger, they needed to have made and implemented key IT infrastructure decisions a long time ago. Because they had made these decisions, the CIO was able to play his role in supporting the company's strategy for purchasing Applebee's.

The business world that we all find ourselves living in these days sure seems to have become more complex. We've got new regulations to live with including Sarbanes-Oxley and General Computing Controls. What all of this means to a business is that IT is now up in front and center of how the business is run. Without including IT in the planning of the company's future direction, there is a great chance that the rest of the company won't be able to find their way...

Chapter 9

Can We Make IT Any More Complex Than It Is?

Chapter 9: Can We Make IT Any More Complex Than It Already Is?

One of the reasons that the rest of the company doesn't seem to really like those of us in the IT department is because we seem to make everything so much more complex when we get involved. First it was our networking issues (Frame Relay, ATM, Ethernet), then it was our server issues (multicore, Intel vs. AMD, caching), and lately it seems to be software design (SaaS, Cloud Computing, Web 2.0). When will this ever end?

Have we screwed things up? Is the CFO and the rest of the financial side of the business correct when they accuse us of buying the latest technology just to play around with it? It turns out, that everyone is probably just a little bit correct this time around.

So here's the scoop: yes, information technology IS becoming more complex. Sorry about that. The reason that IT is becoming more complex is because the world in which we work is becoming more complex. I mean think about it, everyone is going global, expanding (yes, even now), and developing new technologies. What's an IT'er to do?

The so-called "traditional" ways of managing IT no longer work. Now to be fair to us, we have made a lot of progress in simplifying the stuff that we already have. We've been hard at work standardizing and consolidating IT infrastructure and it's starting to show results. But then there's that SOA thing...

Server and storage virtualization has definitely been a double edged sword. It has reduced the number of boxes that we manage, but how we manage the ones that we've got has become more complex. The same can be said for all of the new-fangled software architectures that we've been dreaming up: SaaS, SoA, Cloud Computing, Web 2.0, etc. These new approaches to assembling software components help us to meet regulatory needs and better ensure data security; however, they sure seem to use an unnecessary number of acronyms to get the job done!

When you introduce mobility into the mix, you've just about sealed the deal. Trying to support a wide range of devices that were never designed to work together, getting legacy apps to talk to mobile devices, and keeping everything secure makes life even more complex.

Great, so the world is becoming more complex, IT is becoming more complex, and everyone thinks that we're just sitting around playing with hi-tech toys. How can we possibly stay on top of all of this complexity? Here are five suggestions on how a hard working IT person can actively keep complexity to a minimum in your life:

1. **Standardize**: Simplify your life by standardizing everything that you can get your hands on. Once you've done this, start to consolidate as much as you can.

2. **Get More Bang For Your Buck**: make sure that you are spending your IT time and money where it's going to produce the greatest return. Too much time spent on the wrong things will just make life that much more complex.

3. **Prune – Don't Cut**: There will always be times when the IT budget needs to be cut back. When these times arrive, don't do wholesale across the board cuts, instead trim projects as needed. You may even boost budgets of critical projects.

4. **Use What You've Got**: Make sure that the rest of the company has access to the IT assets that you already have. Putting information online and providing access

to enhanced analytical tools can go a long way in showing IT's value to the rest of the organization.

5. **Outsource Only When Necessary**: Outsourcing does not simplify things, rather it creates more management complexity. If you are too quick to outsource work, then you'll find yourself sitting on top of a management nightmare.

Chapter 10

Welcome To A New Year: Does IT Matter This Year?

Chapter 10: Welcome To A New Year: Does IT Matter This Year?

I'm not sure if you remember, but way back in 2003 Nicholas Carr wrote a piece for the Harvard Business Review called "IT Doesn't Matter". Man-o-Man did this set off a firestorm in the IT community – it was sorta like someone calling your sister ugly. However, time has passed since then and so perhaps it's a good time to stop for a moment and ask ourselves, was Carr right after all?

Carr's point at the time was that the tools of IT have become so standardized and available to everyone that IT can no longer provide a company with a competitive advantage. At first glance, it looks like he's got a good point here.

What do we spend most of our time on today? Keeping things up and running, meeting legal compliance issues, and trying to reduce IT costs. Sure doesn't seem like there is a lot of innovation going on there.

The arrival of Cloud computing and web-based services such as Salesforce.com seem to drive the point home even further – anybody can get their hands on the same sets of IT services. So are we just technicians these days?

Well hold on just a moment, all may not be as bleak as it seems at first. Jeanne Harris over at Accenture is the author of a book called **Competing on Analytics: The New Science of Winning** in which she makes a couple of good points.

It turns out that some companies know how to use IT to get value. Some don't. If you average out all companies, then you end up with a result that says that companies don't get much value from IT. Harris points out that what Carr seems to be missing is that many firms do get a lot of value out of IT because they know how to use it.

Given all of this, here is a quick list of firms that "get" IT and have been putting it to good use. Yes, the components that they are using are available to everyone; it's how they are using it that makes the difference:

1. **Walmart**: has used IT tools to create set of a supply chain management applications that has allowed it to grow to occupy the top spot on Fortune's top 500 list of largest firms.

2. **FedEx:** used IT tools to create an integrated package tracking system that allowed it to offer greater visibility to its customers and thus zoomed by UPS to become the world's biggest cargo airline.

3. **Citibank:** used the new technology of ATMs to double its share of the New York City market back in the early 1980's.

4. **American Airlines:** used its inside IT resources to create the SABRE computerized airline reservation system that went on to become an industry standard.

5. **Harrah's Entertainment**: IT has been used to create their Total Rewards customer tracking database and their Fast Cash real-time incentive gambling management program.

6. **Toyota Motor Corp**: IT has been used to create their just-in-time supply chain and its associated management systems.

7. **Exxon Mobile Corp**: IT is being used to help search for the oil and gas deposits that are becoming increasing

hard to find.

8. **Proctor & Gamble:** IT provides the analytical tools that are needed for data mining that is required to track product sales and adjust pricing and promotions.

9. **Boston Red Sox:** use IT to perform sophisticated data analysis of players, stadiums, other teams, and salaries in order to remain competitive.

Well there you go. In the end, Carr makes a good point – lots of IT shops are making the investment into IT hardware and software; however, they aren't getting any real benefits from this investment. However, there is a subset of firms that are using those generic IT parts to build tools that help them to be highly competitive.

Chapter 11

3 Ways To Fix An IT Department (Suggestions From Europe)

Chapter 11: 3 Ways To Fix An IT Department (Suggestions From Europe)

Kuppinger Cole + Partner (KCP) is a European consulting firm that specializes in identity management. So it goes without saying that they spend their time in and out of multiple IT departments on a daily basis. They know all of our dirty little secrets. One of their founders, Martin Kuppinger has been doing some thinking about how to fix IT departments...

Martin starts out his thinking with some pretty basic suggestions. Specifically, he thinks that IT should be limited in what tasks it performs: do what the company wants you to do and nothing else. Now he follows this up with some clarification: an IT department needs to be able to support new business initiatives, provide insights on how the company is running, and keep itself lean and mean.

I'm pretty much in agreement with Martin, except for one thing. IT is not like accounting: in IT things change and they have a tendency to change quickly. I believe that an IT department has a responsibility to always be pushing the envelope and trying out new things before the rest of the company does. How can you roll a Wiki service out to the company if the folks in IT have not played around with it for a while in order to get to know its ins and outs?

Martin goes on to suggest that IT should be reorganized. He's got some interesting thoughts here. He's recommending that strategy be done in house by the IT department.

Next he starts to whip out the acronyms like GRC (governance, risk management and compliance) when he says that part of IT needs to be keeping an eye on how the business is being run and providing reports to all who need them. Finally, he suggests that IT knowledge be decentralized and placed in the business organizations.

I'm going to go both ways here. I'm not sure if IT needs its own stand-alone strategy department. Instead, I believe that IT needs to participate in the strategy planning that is being done for the whole company. What I think is needed is an architecture department that the IT part of the strategy team reports to.

I'm all for having part of IT monitor the business and provide the business with the reports on how it is performing. This is a critical resource that too many businesses don't know how to do well.

Finally, I think that Martin might be on to something when he suggests that parts of IT should be moved out and into the actual departments that we support. I'm always for getting closer to the customer. There are some tricky questions here about who these IT staffers would report to and how they would be evaluated at the end of the year.

Martin ends up talking about the need for a layer to exist between IT and the rest of the business. His thinking here is that what's been missing from IT is some sort of business control by which IT can be managed.

Once again, I think that he's got some interesting ideas here, but I think that he's missing the mark. I always get nervous when I hear people talking about "layers" because that sure doesn't seem like the best way to streamline an organization. I do agree that an effective way for IT and the rest of the business to communicate is needed.

My thinking on how best to do that is where Martin and I differ. I believe that he's hoping that implementation of standardization will result in smooth communications. I beg to differ. At the end of the day, communication will only occur if the proper motivations are put in place to help it along.

My thinking goes like this: I believe that IT should be judged on results – how did IT's actions help the rest of the business to succeed? Likewise, I think that part of the way that the rest of the business should be judged is on how well they used the tools and information that IT provided them with.

Chapter 12

How Can You Make Your IT Department Strategic?

Chapter 12: How Can You Make Your IT Department Strategic?

Isn't that the goal of every IT department – to move from being viewed as a support organization to somehow becoming part of the company's strategic core? Although we all know that this is what we want, for some reason it sure seems to be very hard to do. Good news – the folks over at Lockheed Martin have figured out how to do it...

Ed Meehan is the VP of operations at Lockheed Martin's Enterprise Information Systems (EIS) and back in 2004 he discovered that he had a problem on his hands. In 1995, Lockheed and Martin Marietta had merged and Ed's IT team had spent the next 10 years consolidating data centers (they actually got to be quite good at it). However, in 2004 they were done and they found themselves adrift – now what should they do?

EIS had neither a strategy nor a focus. Does any of this sound familiar to you? In order to have a strategy, you need to have a goal and since EIS is an internal IT organization they don't have the normal measures of profit and loss. What's an IT department to do?

What EIS had to do was identify a goal, create a strategy to reach that goal, and then sell the strategy to a spread out IT department that had never needed to have a strategy. How hard could that be?

Ed was smart enough to know that he needed to have his team pick the direction that they wanted to go in. He showed up at a meeting with three different popular business books that had three different business strategy goals: become a product leader, become the low-cost leader, or provide complete customer satisfaction. Pick one – you can't do all three. Ed's team picked providing complete customer satisfaction with the customer being Lockheed Martin's internal employees.

So now what? Ed set up an 8-person team who had to map out the new strategy and then get the message out to the rest of the department. Their first step was to create a strategy map which showed how each part of the company would be measured against the goal of providing complete customer satisfaction.

Now the 8-person team couldn't do this alone, so they asked each business unit to design their own strategy map with the thought that once they had this, EIS could then build a master map. You can imagine how well this went over – none of the business departments saw any value in adding strategy to their IT department and so they were, to say the least, reluctant to participate.

The 8-person team didn't give up and they brought Ed in when needed. In the end, they got what they were looking for – a complete map of what it would take to fully satisfy the rest of the company.

Now came the hard part: selling the concept of thinking about the new strategy to the rest of the IT department. The biggest problem turned out to be the middle managers – they had "This Too Shall Pass" syndrome. They figured that they could just wait things out and this "new idea" would go away just like all the other ones before it.

Well, they were wrong. It took a year to get the program off the ground and then it took another year to get the message out and train the staff. However, through relentless communication, they finally did it – everyone bought it.

Lockheed Martin has seen measurable improvements in their operations since this strategy was implemented. Internal customers have rated alignment between divisions as having improved by 160%. Probably the greatest payoff is that at Lockheed Martin, IT is now seen as being strategic.

It's from the forge of failure that the steel of success is formed.

Hard Work Does Not Guarantee Success, But Success Does Not Happen Without Hard Work.

- Dr. Jim Anderson

Create IT Departments That Are Productive And A Valuable Asset To The Rest Of The Company !

Dr. Jim Anderson is available to provide training and coaching on the topics that are the most important to people who have to manage IT departments: how can I build a productive IT department (and keep it together) while at the same time providing the rest of the company with the IT services that they need?

Dr. Anderson believes that in order to both learn and remember what he says, speakers need to laugh. Each one of his speeches is full of fun and humor so that what he says "sticks" with everyone.

Dr. Anderson's CIO Skills Training Includes:

1. How to identify and attract the right type of IT workers to your IT department.
2. How to build relationships with the company's senior management in order to get the support that you need?
3. How to stay on top of changing technology and security issues so that you never get surprised?

Dr. Jim Anderson works with over 100 customers per year. To invite Dr. Anderson to work with you, contact him at:

Phone: 813-418-6970 or
Email: jim@BlueElephantConsulting.com

Photo Credits:

Cover - By: SamsungTomorrow
https://www.flickr.com/photos/samsungtomorrow/

Chapter 1 - By: Amber MacPherson
https://www.flickr.com/photos/ambergris/

Chapter 2 – By: priyanphoenix
http://www.morguefile.com/archive/display/729987

Chapter 3 – By: Kabedi Fernando
https://www.flickr.com/photos/95699844@N08/

Chapter 4 – By: Blatant World
https://www.flickr.com/photos/blatantworld/

Chapter 5 – By: hepingting
https://www.flickr.com/photos/57570482@N06/

Chapter 6 – By: Éole Wind
https://www.flickr.com/photos/eole/

Chapter 7 – By: Ed Yourdon
https://www.flickr.com/photos/yourdon/

Chapter 8 – By: Mike Mozart
https://www.flickr.com/photos/jeepersmedia/

Chapter 9 – By: Neal Jennings
https://www.flickr.com/photos/sweetone/

Chapter 10 – By: Jon Scheiber
https://www.flickr.com/photos/winmac/

Chapter 11 – By: Cemre
https://www.flickr.com/photos/f/

Chapter 12 – By: Charles Atkeison
https://www.flickr.com/photos/atkeison/

Other Books By The Author

Product Management

- How Product Managers Can Grow Their Career: How Product Managers Can Find And Succeed In The Right Job

- Product Management Secrets: Techniques For Product Managers To Boost Product Sales And Increase Customer Satisfaction

- Product Development Lessons For Product Managers: How Product Managers Can Create Successful Products

- Customer Lessons For Product Managers: Techniques For Product Managers To Better Understand What Their Customers Really Want

- Product Failure Lessons For Product Managers: Examples Of Products That Have Failed For Product Managers To Learn From

- Communication Skills For Product Managers: The Communication Skills That Product Managers Need To Know How To Use In Order To Have A Successful Product

- How To Have A Successful Product Manager Career: The Things That You Need To Be Doing TODAY In Order To Have A Successful Product Manager Career

- Product Manager Product Success: How to keep your product on track and make it become a success

Public Speaking

- How To Organize A Successful Speech: How to put together a speech that will clearly communicate your message to your audience

- How To Become A Better Speaker By Changing How You Speak: Change techniques that will transform a speech into a memorable event

- How To Give A Great Presentation: Presentation techniques that will transform a speech into a memorable event

- How To Rehearse In Order To Give The Perfect Speech: How to effectively rehearse your next speech to that your message be remembered forever!

- Secrets To Creating The Perfect Speech: How to create a speech that will make your message be remembered forever!

- Secrets To Organizing The Perfect Speech: How to organize the best speech of your life!

- Secrets To Planning The Perfect Speech: How to plan to give the best speech of your life

- How To Show What You Mean During A Presentation: How to use visual techniques to transform a speech into a memorable event

CIO Skills

- What CIOs Need To Know About Working With Partners: Techniques For CIOs To Use In Order To Be Able To Successfully Work With Partners

- Critical CIO Management Skills: Decision Making Skills That Every CIO Needs To Have In Order To Be Able To Make The Right Choices

- How CIOs Can Make Innovation Happen: Tips And Techniques For CIOs To Use In Order To Make Innovation Happen In Their IT Department

- CIO Communication Skills Secrets: Tips And Techniques For CIOs To Use In Order To Become Better Communicators

- Managing Your CIO Career: Steps That CIOs Have To Take In Order To Have A Long And Successful Career

- CIO Business Skills: How CIOs can work effectively with the rest of the company!

IT Manager Skills

- How IT Managers Can Make Innovation Happen: Tips And Techniques For IT Managers To Use In Order To Make Innovation Happen In Their Teams

- Staffing Skills IT Managers Must Have: Tips And Techniques That IT Managers Can Use In Order To Correctly Staff Their Teams

- Secrets Of Effective Leadership For IT Managers: Tips And Techniques That IT Managers Can Use In Order To Develop Leadership Skills

- IT Manager Career Secrets: Tips And Techniques That IT Managers Can Use In Order To Have A Successful Career

- IT Manager Budgeting Skills: How IT Managers Can Request, Manage, Use, And Track Their Funding

<u>Negotiating</u>

- Learn How To Signal In Your Next Negotiation: How To Develop The Skill Of Effective Signaling In A Negotiation In Order To Get The Best Possible Outcome

- Learn The Skill Of Exploring In A Negotiation: How To Develop The Skill Of Exploring What Is Possible In A Negotiation In Order To Reach The Best Possible Deal

- Learn How To Argue In Your Next Negotiation: How To Develop The Skill Of Effective Arguing In A Negotiation In Order To Get The Best Possible Outcome

- How To Open Your Next Negotiation: How To Start A Negotiation In Order To Get The Best Possible Outcome

- Preparing For Your Next Negotiation: What You Need To Do BEFORE A Negotiation Starts In Order To Get The Best Possible Deal

Miscellaneous

- Software Defined Networking: Design and Deployment, CRC Press 2014

- The Internet-Enabled Successful School District Superintendent: How To Use The Internet To Boost Parental Involvement In Your Schools

- Power Distribution Unit (PDU) Secrets: What Everyone Who Works In A Data Center Needs To Know!

- Making The Jump: How To Land Your Dream Job When You Get Out Of College!

How CIOs Can Use Their Technical Skills To Help Their Company Solve Real-World Business Problems

This book has been written with one goal in mind – to show you how you use the great technical skills that you have to help your company solve the business problems that they are facing. Learn how to use what you know to help your company move faster and do more!

Let's Make Your CIO Career A Success!

What You'll Find Inside:

- **10 WAYS THAT IT CAN SOLVE REAL-WORLD BUSINESS PROBLEMS**
- **ARE CIOS LOOKING DOWN WHEN THEY SHOULD BE LOOKING UP?**
- **3 WAYS TO FIX AN IT DEPARTMENT (SUGGESTIONS FROM EUROPE)**
- **HOW CAN YOU MAKE YOUR IT DEPARTMENT STRATEGIC**

Dr. Jim Anderson brings his 25 years of real-world experience to this book. He's been a senior IT executive at some of the world's largest firms. He's going to show you what you need to do (and not do!) in order to make your CIO career a success!

www.ingramcontent.com/pod-product-compliance
Lightning Source LLC
Chambersburg PA
CBHW071801170526
45167CB00003B/1123